Seasonings

Seasonings

Emilio DeGrazia

NODIN PRESS

Copyright © 2012 EmilioDeGrazia, all rights reserved. No part of this book may be reproduced in any form without permission in writing from Nodin Press, except for purposes of review.

ISBN: 978-1-935666-41-7
Library of Congress Control Number: 2011945350
Cover art is based on a painting, "Persephone," by Julie Crozier of Winona, Minnesota. Photograph by Michelle Kowaleski. Thank you to Larry and Colleen Wolner of the Blue Heron Coffee Shop, Winona, for the use of Julie Crozier's work.

Design: John Toren

ACKNOWLEDGEMENTS
The poems in this collection, several of them revised, originally appeared in the literary magazines and anthologies listed below.

"Best Men," *Italian Americana* (2004). "Conservations," *Heterodoxy* (1987). Reprinted in *Pivot* (1990). "Fifth Grade Band Concert," *Lake Street Review* (1987). "Good Friday Blue," *West Branch* (1989). "Good Friday (2005)," *Green Blade* (2006). "Gospel Hour in the Nursing Home," *Tenth Annual Poet-Artist Collaboration* (Crossings at Carnegie, 2011.) "Great Battles of the Century," *Poetic Strokes* (2009). "Horn Call," *The Horn Call* (2009). "I Lay My Case Before Him," *Once in a Sycamore: A Garland for John Berryman* (Rook, 1976). Reprinted in *Loonfeather* (1989). "Late Autumn Repairs," *Northfield Magazine* (1992). "Moving Without the Ball," *Minnesota Monthly* (1994). "Night Music," *Loonfeather* (1989). "Pasttime," *This Sporting Life* (Milkweed, 1987). Reprinted in *As Far as I Can See: Contemporary Writing of the Middle Plains* (Windflower, 1989), and in *Reading and Writing Poetry with Teenagers* (Walch, 1996), and in *Just Buffalo* (Buffalo, N.Y. Literary Center, 1999). "Pitcher," *Fan Magazine* (1992). Reprinted in *Elysian Fields* (1992). "Professor of Desire," *Carleton Miscellany* (1979). "Recipe," originally published as "Bittersweet Green" in *Writers Who Cook* (Herringbone Press, 1994). "Rainbow Man," *Laurel Review* (1990). "Reading Between the Lines," *Black Bear Review* (1991). "Retributions," *Hiram Poetry Review* (1986). Reprinted in *Piedmont Literary Review* (1986). "River Town," *Mankato Poetry Review* (1989). Reprinted in *Phoenix* (1989). "Serenade," *Turtle Quest* (2009). "Snow Day," *The Other Side* (1990). Reprinted in *Pivot* (1990). "The Day the Rollercoaster Stopped," *2AM Magazine* (1989). Reprinted in *Agazziz Review* (1989). "The Fallen in Battle," *Green Blade* (2009). "The Lessons of History," *Sarajevo Project Anthology* (1993). Reprinted in *Through a Child's Eyes* (PlainView Press, 2001). "Tennis Lessons," *Cimarron Review* (1986). Reprinted in *Families in Transition* (McGraw-Hill, 1993) and *The Tie That Binds* (Papier Mache, 1989). "Vatican Parts," *ArtWord Quarterly* (1997). "Visitations," *Green Blade* (2006).

Nodin Press
530 N 3rd Street
Suite 120
Mpls, MN, 55401

To Monica
For her serene intelligence
and gracious love

Contents

HE LOVED MORNINGS BEST

13 / Apologia
13 / The Voices He Hears
14 / Old Math
15 / What Leaves Know
16 / Thaw
17 / Returns
17 / Influence
18 / Visitations
19 / Gospel Hour in the Nursing Home
20 / Good Friday Blue (1986)
21 / Good Friday (April 1, 1994)
22 / Good Friday (2005)
23 / Best Men
24 / The Disappearance of Bees
25 / The Work of Her Hands
26 / Vatican Parts
27 / Why Unicorns Hide
28 / Fifth Grade Band Concert
29 / First Period
30 / Girl at Her Piano
31 / Twentieth Century Son
31 / Ode to Joy

WHERE SHADOWS AND SUN DIVIDE

35 / Mississippi River Town
36 / Dentist's Chair
37 / Tennis Lessons
38 / Night Music
39 / Summer Storm

40 / Sunday Drive
41 / The Lessons of History
42 / Ontologies
43 / Rachel, as Leah
44 / Love Math
45 / Horn Call
46 / Geology
47 / Mothers of the Sons
48 / Stolen Kid's Bike
49 / Serenade
50 / Prayer Meetings
51 / Life after Death
51 / Referents
52 / Home Run
53 / Jar
54 / The Book of the Dead
55 / Food Thoughts
56 / Making Eyes
57 / Ratification
58 / Legacy
59 / Winona
60 / Windup
60 / Pastime

BEDS OF LEAVES ON FOREST FLOOR

62 / September Song
63 / Blind Date
64 / Declaration of War
65 / The Fallen in Battle
66 / Recreations
67 / Recipe
68 / Great Battles of the Century
68 / So Gardens Die
69 / An Eschatology
69 / Perfumes
70 / Jane Fonda Worked Out

71 / Strip-Search
71 / October Day
72 / Four Freedoms
73 / If Thine Eye Offend Thee
74 / Still Lives
75 / Nuns' Cemetery
75 / Weeds
76 / Late Autumn Repairs

THE BOTTOM OF THE NINTH

79 / The Day the Rollercoaster Stopped
80 / Empty Country Church
81 / "I Lay My Case Before Him"
82 / Wagner's Valkyrie
83 / After the Logging
84 / Of Maps
85 / The Riddle of the Sphinx
86 / Circulations
87 / Jesus at Home
88 / The Third Gift
89 / Christmas Carol 1999
90 / Day after Christmas
91 / Moving without the Ball
92 / Rainbow Man
93 / Home Alone
94 / Retirement How-To
96 / Palimpsest
97 / Snow Day
98 / The Thirteenth Month
100 / The Meaning of Life

❧ HE LOVED MORNINGS BEST

APOLOGIA

The big-hipped clerk in the hardware store
Limps to her post at the cash register.
There my art is required to wait in line
For her to perform her check-out work.

Standing ahead of me a true-blue friend
Nails my core with her hard truth:
"Those vague poems the boys call art—
They're self-indulgent noise."

I lurk past the edges of the clerk's worn smile
And hear the dark timbre of her voice.
I never ask: Do you read poetry?
I muse: We both need music more.

THE VOICES HE HEARS

When he was told to find his voice
He stood still as a wild deer, ears erect
For hints of death's whisperings
About the unspoken presence of his life.

Leaves quiver as thoughts breeze past
A sky overcast with regrets repeated like lines
Of a dreary old hymn hummed in his ear
By a fly zeroing in on a drumbeat heart
Insanely dancing around a crackling fire
Moths on unsteady wings find beautiful.

In this choired symphony
Where is the certain steady voice?
When undertows serenade the flights of gulls
While waters beat rhythms on floating rocks,
What solitary singer is a soloist?

OLD MATH

The seagulls who abandon their beach
And commute the fifty miles
Above the currents of the New Jersey coast
To dine six days a week at the Newark dump

Never calculate if the calorie count
Required to make the return flights
To their lazy seaside resorts
Is worth their daily journey to the feast.

Nor has anyone figured
What tonnage of human debris
They translate into a glide of wings
Wise enough to navigate

The wandering mind of winds
That know no rest on Sunday morns
When the dump is chained shut,
Or how that ensemble of gulls,

Drawing their own figures in sky,
Knows enough about holiday time
To wing it every seventh day at home.

WHAT LEAVES KNOW

The power of place,
Their role
In the dazzling outcome of roots.

The art of living within view
Of the two fragrances of life,
Sun and shade.

The politics of free passage
For air allied to no state.

The turn the other cheek tactic
For storms gone wild.

How to brew the air we crave.

How to orchestrate
The incomparable music
Composed by anonymous wind.

Leaves know how to sway
And dance,
How to put their colors on,
Blaze away, be

Outward and visible signs
Of a big beautiful thing
Wonderfully in the way.

On foggy still nights
They know the atonement of sleep,

The moment to let go.

THAW

Two old men on the April park bench
Nitpick each other's stories
Until the bag lady in between
Silences them with bananas for everyone,
The biggest for herself.

As they peel and dig in,
The patches of snow beneath trees
(Still bare except for leftover leaves
hanging by a thread)
Are warmed by odors rising
From the collars of their overcoats.

So when there is no more nitpicking
To be done, no quips to delouse,
Snow softens on April sod
For bananas eaten quietly in good time.

RETURNS

Only the sailboat's mind is full enough
To feel flesh quivering inside
The Great Plain grass ground to silence
In the wake of Progress' high ways,

And only sailors longing for home
Smell the fragrant sheets of gray rain
Above sea meadows
Where husks grainy as hulls turn up each spring.

INFLUENCE

By the time we tasted the rumors in canned milk
The cows had gone mad,
And farmers, crazed by the price of corn,
Wandered lost in parking ramps.

Nobody knew how fog could stain
the faces of porcelain dolls,
Or how bad air, once in, could ever be aired out.

VISITATIONS

The stranger came from south of all borders,
From a village flooded every spring
When the waters of the Sea of Galilee turn black.
He smelled of garlic, sweat and fish,
And hair danced like seaweed on his back.

"Let me do this or that for you," he said.
"I'm alone in a doorway looking out.
Let me tell stories to your kids,
Change your motor oil to water,
And help you wipe the stains
From the windows of your church."

His tongue untwisted their words—
So they bunked him in outhouse shacks
Where motel maids and carwashers
Don't amount to a hill of beans,
And where their white wives would never see
To the bottom of eyes so brown.

GOSPEL HOUR IN THE NURSING HOME

Ah sunflowers!
All you ladies in waiting in the nursing home
Cradling your heavy heads in your own laps
As the TV preacher
Delivers his message
Bottled in the TV tube,

If you could imagine a heaven
Where everyone walks in slow-motion time
Along the streets you knew by heart
With the children you knew by name,
Sons and daughters strolling past,
Newborns asleep on fragrant sheets,
Nameless lovers marching down marriage aisles
To the doors you opened a crack
Hoping to find yourself in a stranger's room
Beautiful again, in your new dress,
The girl you once were,
The women you never became—

Then this rebirth is worth waiting for,
Your ear listening for the faint pulse of sea,
As you gaze far out at the waters
Breaking for you and the head in your lap,
Your newborn child.

GOOD FRIDAY BLUE
(1986)

After the Catechism, Communion, Confirmation,
The hardening of trust into truth,
We expected rain Good Friday afternoons.

No baseball then, no playing in streets,
No kicking the can, no
Playing robbers or war
Those painful hours from noon to three.

In those days we always saw the evidence: Rain,
A steady stream of punishment,
The Holy Spirit's drizzle descending like ash,
Or wayward bursts, big as water balloons,
Dropped from passing clouds
Flying in formation overhead,
A certain proof of God.

Today, that April day again
When the only gospel is the same old news,
The dying still goes on.
But the sky is faultlessly blue,
An Easter sky ahead of its times,
One more kind of progress to endure.
In such skies old deaths
Have happened once and for all,
And new ones everywhere provide
Too much space to agonize.

GOOD FRIDAY
(April 1, 1994)

Jesus speaks:

This year I have it my way:
My day—the rose-red three hours
I spend trying to hang on—
Double-featured with the agony
Of everyday fools.

If I were unreal I could try you again
With my spectacular wet jokes:
My walking-on-water routine,
My conversion of runoff to wine,
Or (in the hi-tech video style required
Of belief), I could cast your demons out
Into unconscious streams.

But oh, if I could lure you close enough
For you to smell my flesh,
My limbs would embrace you
With a simple truth:
That once upon a time
There were countless fools
Nameless like me, rooted,
Hung up on this or that,
Reaching for sky,
Unleaving.

GOOD FRIDAY
(2005)

The need to garden came on suddenly
After the elephants ate all the grass
Then lay down and died
Next to palm trees dropping leaves
As the crippled vultures
With two right wings
Stood by and squawked.

First I did away with the fence
To allow the moon to circulate
Into the cracks of caked mud
Where beetles scurry to escape
The nightmares inside office eyes.

Then I stripped the graveyards
Bare of old bones, whistling
As I flung them to the wind.

At last I raked in lust,
Heaped it into a pyre
On the village square,
Then coaxed my old mother
Out of her cave toward the blaze.

I watched the flames all night,
Still awake at dawn
To see her ashes
Dark as Eve's skin
Drift toward the humming of bees.

BEST MEN
(At the wedding of my sister Beatrice)

When the Colonel appeared as best man
The altar took a vow of silence
And the choir stonewalled a salute
To my sister, the bride, all white.

Beatrice—you who loved to dance
With your weeping willow hair
Over the lilies of the field
Through the nine circles of sky—

Who is this man you stand to wed
Whose best man is beside himself
In crewcut authority *semper fidelis*
To do naming of parts?

The blood of conquered tribes
Swirls in this new love-stew of yours.
Now you marry the Colonel too,
The ribbons that flower on his breast,
The medals heavy as chains of the blessed,
Each an emblem of uniform deaths.

THE DISAPPEARANCE OF BEES
(Beatrice, musician d. April 27, 2007)

I listen for their humming
In the May Day mourning's quietest hour,
For their music shimmering like a veil
Over the pear tree's white blossoming.

My sister Beatrice, so suddenly gone,
Her thin smile forced onto the *papier-mâche*
Of her hard painted face.
Not one bee hums a tune
In the dense odors of funeral flowers.

And even bee carcasses are gone,
Disappeared. Suddenly nobody home.
What resurrection can we hope for
When the final pear falls from the tree?
Her lovely music here is stilled,
While late April blossoms wait like abandoned brides.

THE WORK OF HER HANDS

The needlepoint that unwound
My mother's years
At the end of exhausted days hid
From all eyes rummaging to buy a fragment
Of redemption in her final estate.

The leftover fabrics of her life
Speak: You're not rid of me yet.
I'm here still, unmoved,
Frayed but not gone
From here, my only place in life, my home.

What to do with abandoned scraps,
The streams of consciousness
She needled into silent designs?
How riddled were the forms her fingers drew
And how many of her pins pierced hearts?

Do we go to the dumpster with them
Or place them in the donation bins
Of our salvation armies and good wills,
These bundles of swaddling cloth,
Foundlings for second-hand hearts?

VATICAN PARTS

In a marble crypt
Beneath Bramante's Corridor
We find the lost Vatican penises
Piled high in a pyramid heap.

In dungeon light the bonewhite hoard
Lopped one by one from the statues above
Glistens like maggots
Twisting and turning in sleep.

If we could touch we would
Find ourselves more in love
With Apollo *Belvedere*, Centocelle's *Eros*,
And a host of statesmen, poets and gods.

But the faithful Nun,
(Demoted Mother Superior
Assigned to keep an eye on it all),
Fingers her beads saying no again no.

In these fractured times,
Noisy with tourist echoes overhead,
She prays, Where is my father,
My lover, the son?

WHY UNICORNS HIDE
(Words come round)

The once upon a time unicorn
Its head God-forever high
Grows out big hard horn
Pointed as it knew
The way to the garden, the green,
The apple especially red, no more shamed
Than mere beautiful thing
Hid in the unicorn's eye

Where once upon a time
The hard mere horny high God
Pointed the green way out,
The garden no more the beautiful thing,
The apple in the eye red
As it grew shamed head
In the way of the horn,
And forever the unicorn hid.

FIFTH GRADE BAND CONCERT
(Mayday, 1986)

Though children still play in the streets of Kiev,
The atmosphere is wronged for this scheduled event.
Faces are scrubbed too clean, and paper flowers,
Pinned-down leftovers from last fall's float,
Droop, and the eyes of manila robins are
Blank, as if big with fear. Something evil exists
In this spring air. Even the curtain quivers,
Palsied by an unseen hand.

The wind outside twists and turns in the dark,
Desperate for any way out, whistling in
Through cracks in windows and doors
Wherever possible. Wherever possible

The unscheduled air above Chernobyl
Lurks invisibly, as a daughter, eyes radiant,
Lifts the clarinet from her knee,
And awaits the command to play
Her first public march.

That blast requires even fathers to notice
These times, the winds and brass
complaining in unison,
Drums the half-life of a heartbeat behind.

In the blare of this dusty hall
Where error also is mechanical,
Merely a human thing,
No valve fails a single heart
Pumping the nameless
Spirit playing itself out,
The only good air.

FIRST PERIOD

A father's old school bell tolls
A diminished tone, time still
Catalogued by subject and authority,
All periods watched over by clocks.

From hour one he dreamed escape
Through windows and doors
Into the wide-open spaces of books,
Their wars all love.

Now you, my girl, have another course
To divide morning from you,
Cramp your innocent style,
And require you to come round

To that womanhood further still
From you now than the blue
Beautiful autumn day you were born
Is from you now.

What old lessons from these new pains?
What could one day come
From this spilling of guts?
Will you taste the earth-blood

Smeared on your hands,
Dream dreaded new forms
And see the child still here,
Smell her clean flesh?

GIRL AT HER PIANO

How difficult this matter is,
Like flesh,
All the piano parts—
Ivory, wood, steel—
Resisting your reluctant hands.

And reluctantly I, father,
Require you to play on,
Practice your art
Fumble your way
Work on your touch
Until you feel
The music and, suddenly
Aroused, it touches you.

Then will your hands
Become the lover's hands,
Rhythms and chords
Coming together
Playing you.

TWENTIETH CENTURY SON

At dawn the men and machines again regroup
To cut down the trees, grind their limbs.
My infant son awakens to the noise,
Cries for his mother to please take him in.

Here he is again, somebody's soldier boy blitzed
By the Black Forest madness all around.
His legs are useless and limp.
His only uniform is nudity.

ODE TO JOY

Today, on the ninth spring day
Of our latest Mideast war,
My seven year-old son
Puts his ear to my heart.

"What do you hear?" I ask.
"It sounds like music in there, Dad,"
He says, lifting his eyes as I conduct
The symphony, on the ninth spring day.

WHERE SHADOWS AND SUN DIVIDE

MISSISSIPPI RIVER TOWN

Here old time remains unmoved,
Here where sandbars tread water
Weightier than local chemistries,
And the heron's lofty silence glides.

And here the earth still holds its ground,
Where life, liberty, and the pursuit
Of property trespass equally.
And in solitary streets citizen-strangers are
Unmoved by roads leading away.

Even the old elm, finally defunct,
Recalls in its browned bones
The once-upon-a-time woods,

And when the blackbird turns its head
Toward horizon of fields and sky,
Fences are an invisible blur.

DENTIST'S CHAIR

In our position, comfortable enough
To inspire dozing off, we refuse to see
What they're doing to us, and can't be sure
If it's right or terribly wrong.

Technically, we're not strapped down,
But the weight of every thing we lack
Requires us to surrender free will here,
A good place to gag on how we vote.

We're certain the doctor has eyes,
And we note hair under his gloved hands.
Behind his mask there's certainly a mouth,
Though his breathing we never hear.

We try to swallow and dare to squirm
As he moves the mirror close
To see what lurks in the caves
Of widespread speechlessness.

We close our eyes until the drill touches
Another twentieth century nerve.
We don't flinch as he removes the gold
And then the teeth, piling them in fat heaps
On frozen fields cut by railroad tracks.

TENNIS LESSONS

When your life was too small
To cast a shadow halfway up my leg,
We did no more than chase the crazy ball.
Spindle-legged like a one-day fawn,
You sat on the concrete and wept.
Once you blasted the ball over the fence,
Then commanded me to retrieve it like a bone:
A shameless power play.

In time you began to respect control.
Though mainly content to skitter, flail away,
You began to feel the ball's perfect pitch,
Bird released from its cage.
It was Shakespeare and Mozart in the round.
By then you were eager to guide
No less than the earth with your hands,
Hide that green apple behind your back,
Dare me to steal it from you.

Tomorrow, with the score forever tied
Love-love, we will spend sunsets gliding
That ball back and forth, back and forth,
Your touch, graced by strong form,
Keeping the play just
Within my failing reach.

NIGHT MUSIC

When you laugh in your sleep
I eavesdrop on your dream,
I, father, locked neither in nor out,
My ear at the door of your heart,
My ear to the ground,
And I on old knees, listening there.

The dream is always ancient and new—
At once song, story, and wedding dance.

In it I am the bear out of the woods,
The burry one in red-feathered shorts
Who tickles small feet with his nose,
Blows words through his ears
And dances polkas on Saturn's rings
Without tilting the windmills in his head.
When he tries to escape from the elephant toads
A fawn traps him in a canning jar,
Punches holes in the top, makes faces at him.

He appears at her window one night,
Nose pressed to the glass,
King Kong big with pity and fear
Until he slips on the sill
And falls on his butt.

As I wait for applause, laughter again,
I hoard all morals to myself:
How you undo fathers everywhere,
How it is all your fault
That Turk jailers give their keys away
And Chilean generals suddenly disarm
And bad husbands return to good wives;
How you bring Arab shepherds to their knees,
Allow them to see in clean night skies
The motions of a melody dancing there

Dressed in a lacework of stars—there too
A father laughing at a crazy bear
Giving bride and her laughter away.

SUMMER STORM

When we heard the news—
El Nino was coming soon—we hid
With a candle and canned goods
In the basement of the soul.

With our ears to the ground
We heard the Valkyrie trains
Screaming in tune with the prayers
Of believers performing their exodus.

That night all the trees,
The wonderful trees,
Obedient to wind's ways, fell.
They fell across streets and railroad tracks.

Nobody could progress.
The trees missed every cottage, barn
And beaver dam, the wonderful trees
That made the trains run late.

SUNDAY DRIVE
(June, 1989)

Once more this day of the sun,
Holy Day, we hone our wheels,
Sure it's all ours, this hour,
World without end,

Centuries sinking as they pass
Into ooze of oil.
Also sunk are the beautiful
Gardens of Babylon,
Crushed with forgotten forests
Into prehistoric sludge
Below desert sands driven
At sixty-five miles per hour
Toward gas station sunset in space,
World without end.

And world without end
The armies keep gearing up,
Nobody measuring
How many miles per gallon
Of Arab boy blood.

THE LESSONS OF HISTORY
(Yugoslavia, 1992-93)

Here in this land the curse
Is crescent-crossed,
All shreds of the argument
Hung up on Truth.
Rivers, clotted with cleansed
Bones of the dead,
Have nowhere to run,
And memory is so vengeance-gorged
It has completely lost its mind.
Where the Sign of the Cross
Has a left and right wing
Chained to armored divisions
Blasting equally to hell
The catholic orthodox infidel;
Where the male is master
When mounting the slave,
Woman and child—then
Assisi, Mecca, and Sarajevo
Are equally the shrines
Of Death Squad saints.

ONTOLOGIES

> *"I almost don't believe in God…"*
> – cousin Louis DeGrazia, theologian

The door leading to a cedar closet
Is open a crack. The blackness inside
Appalls the wallpaper, curtains, and sunlight.

On the porch an old man rocks, humming,
While Beatrice, lovely in the living room,
Dances fingers over piano keys.
The bees, singing circles in mid-air,
Prepare the way for the fulfillment
Of the prophecies of Johnny Appleseed
Blossoming in the neighbor's yard.
Two dimes rattle inside the beggar-bum's cup.
A cousin prepares another feast,
And mothers love their children
To the nth degree.

RACHEL, AS LEAH

Rachel, hiding under Jacob's bed,
Could not help herself, her animal ears
Alert for Leah's breathed whisperings
To her silent surrogate God.

Better nothing said. Best if Leah,
That sacred cow, Rachel's representative,
Were alone in her own chamber too,
Dreaming the serenity of the freshly bred.

Still, what wouldn't Rachel do
To be in Leah's place,
Her eyes half-aware
Of the bonewhite glow
Of some altar sacrifice scene,
Feeling just once each careless thrust
Of her Lord's great lust, her hands
Loving him, oh, so skin-deep.

LOVE MATH

You ask if I love other women too.
My solemn word adds up to no and yes.
Since no single woman can equal you
The heart's new math concludes that more is less.

If I can lie with you why would I lie
With the brilliant babe, those magic eyes,
Or with the lonelyheart who just dropped by
Or tease who leaves me in a wake of sighs,

Or sexy chick who can't say no,
Or careful nurse hot for a slow ride
When rage and gloom have no sane place to go?
Why multiply when there is no divide?

Another woman alone will never do,
For all the world's choice women are in you.

HORN CALL

What words of objection can a father air
When a daughter abandons her grand old piano
To become consort of a new French Horn?

She, whose hands might have made
Salons resonate with categorical imperatives
Sounding the pure reason of her whims.

Debussy now stands jilted in cold rain,
Recalling how her fingertip touch
Sent shivers over his skin.

For she is bright goddess now,
Queen of gleaming serpent and circled womb,
Mermaid in chambered nautilus
With blossoming conch golden-eared.

What is she making of herself
From the blood and guts her horn of plenty
Sounds through speechless lips?

The lovely music her hands
Once unlocked with the piano keys
Now gathers in her breast

Where love, beauty and the hunt
Sink and soar with the winds.

GEOLOGY

That one true mother of yours—
Who? In you, daughter,
The one handed down? You
Given up, adopted at birth
By empty-roomed strangers
Too soon divorced
From each other, divided,
Dividing you?

Now in the weaning
Will you seek some others out—
Sister step-nurse offering
Her heart in her hands, breasts
As full as the earth is
Continuous with you?

If so, look for me, father, there too,
Wholly gay in the loving of you,
All girl and mother too.

MOTHERS OF THE SONS

Today the mothers are wailing again.
Yesterday's war by their bloody sons
Left grief on their hands and sheets.

How did issues one night
So suddenly turn red
For these makers of men again forced
To wash from plain flesh
Familiar blood stain?

As war's hot blades burn new pain
On the walls of women's wombs,
They skew the old cycle
And remake mothers
Into successors of sons.

STOLEN KID'S BIKE
(July 4, 1999)

The consolation is historical:
By stealth the American Revolution
Takes another sly step
Toward its evolutionary end—
The indivisible right of have-nots
To equal the haves.

Because the sky was sunny all day,
Because I have two bikes,
And my lawn is cut clean.

Because children in mud villages sleep
With hunger wheeling in their guts.

Because their grandmothers' eyes
Are vigilant and fierce.

SERENADE

In the still moment
Before darkness and sleep,
Wind, having nowhere to go,
Settles into the quietness
Of the evening neighborhood.

Progress has no place in this calm.
Lovers stroll past uselessly
Offering nothing for sale,
And boys gaze beyond cars
Lining the streets with nowhere to go.

Here, in the heart's small home,
A mirror whispers secrets to a face
Believing it becomes lovelier
As long smooth hair
Glides like water through a comb.
And there, on the porch beyond the lawn
Shadowed by a silver maple tree,
A swing sways back and forth
On end-rhymed air.

PRAYER MEETINGS

In the palm grove
Where hippo and gazelle
Drink from the same pond,
There is no holy war.

When serpent and dove
Eye each other in the same tree,
There is no love or hate.
There is no creed.

From the grass where lion
And jackal lie low,
Hunger springs of necessity.
There God, embarrassed, hides too.

In churches where Christian
Soldiers bring in the sheaves
There is belief and, of necessity,
An approving God
And his angel hosts, all ghosts.

LIFE AFTER DEATH

On the night of the execution the lights dimmed
In Beijing, Atlanta, and Kabul.
The people shivering in markets and shops
Looked for ways to escape
Through the cracks of windows and doors,
While those hurrying home from jobs
Pulled shadows over their heads to keep warm.

In all the schools the newest math proclaimed
Zero times one
Minus dreams to the nth power
Is equal to the common denominator.
The remainder remains unsaid.

REFERENTS

To behead a flower
Is not,
As the poet chimed,
To make love.

To take one from two,
If we completely count,
Leaves us with one
Or three.

"To kill a man,"
The heretic Castellio said,
"Is not to defend
A doctrine,
But to kill a man."

HOME RUN

Here I am, my fingers gripping
The chain-link backstop fence
With the game not really close
And my twelve year-old kid at bat

With the count three and two,
When the damned phone rings in
Some appointment not kept
With someone trying to score a buck.

How dare you,
Just as the ball crosses the plate
High,
And I agree yes, way too high,

Besides he's small for his age,
So he walked, no

He's running to the base, no
You walked, I command you

Walk, don't go so fast.
It's called a walk,

No hurrying to any base.
I want to see every move,

Every small step,
With you standing

There on first,
Safe.

JAR

As the waters rose
Past his knees and hips,
He shivered with the thrill
Of being so fulfilled,
And lost all fear.

On the road home the vessel
Weighed heavily on his mind,
His pace an uncertain sway
Past the leering marketplace.

In the shade he loved
The curve and cool and sweat
Of the thing, the way his palms felt
Around its rough clay.

And when the crowd required him
To mix the water and wine,
He loved how everything spilled
Through his fingers
To the ground.

THE BOOK OF THE DEAD

In the grass
The beetle reads
Her way
Over the sand
To the small hole
Where shadows
And sun divide.

There the beetle
Is
Seasoned
For a time
That is all
Time
Beyond belief
And too secure
To interest any
High heroes
Or gods.

FOOD THOUGHTS

My hungry mind, that hive of sponge-caked files,
Can't look the other way, somehow ignore
The feast of facts the curious eye compiles
To feed the greedy soul, that omnivore.

Nor can my daily bread and wine keep pace
With courses of science and banquets of art
Served to unfit winners of the human race
Who choke down ignorance to grow less heart.

When I see flies feed on children's eyes
And war's bloody bodies bloated with belief,
The news, that marathon of spinning lies,
Runs me down as I run from grief.

With legs gone dumb and care hard as stone
I hide from what I know, and feast alone.

MAKING EYES

A starling assaults the window of the train
Speeding me to God knows where.
Trying desperately to keep up,
The bird strikes again and is gone.

In front of me the old black man sleeps
In his torn shirt, hat over his eyes.
From across the aisle the pretty Asian girl
Glares permanently at the border guard.

I have taken too much from them.
What can I give back?

RATIFICATION
(Dedication of the Winona State University Library)

Here, in the solemn silence
Of these democratic walls stilled
By a congress of voices ratifying
Our theft of fire from oppressive gods
And once-forbidden compulsion
To discern the difference
Between evil and good,
Here we ask forgiveness
Of this blameless ground
Once graced by grass and trees
And the enduring logic of wind.

Our duty here is to handle with care
The leaves scholars script,
And reply in truth to diviners
Of fossil, atom and galaxy,
Critics, dreamers, computers, and sage
Fools who dare to speak against
The sophists who pay their way in.

Our good in this sanctuary honors
Those with eyes in their hearts
And ears for the cries
Of the voiceless weak, victims
Of that knowledge and power
Now also present, here.

On these dedicated grounds
Where grass and trees no longer breathe
In the enduring logic of wind,
Abandon all fear of hope
Only ye who enter here
With pride rooted in humility.

LEGACY
*(Naming of the Darrell W. Krueger Library,
Winona State University)*

If the man for whom we name this space
Would speak for himself
He would not say, "Honor me."
He would point to the words engraved in stone—
In libris libertas—
Then open his arms to these doors,
Welcome us to the quiet
That speaks volumes here,
The windows that shatter noise
As they let in the light.

Here, in a troubled world,
A dream endures: In this serenity
The life of the mind awakens
The compassionate creativity
Civil societies require to carry on.
Here we earn entrance to the new ignorance
All knowledge reveals as new mystery.
We come here to authenticate ourselves,
Validate the stories by which we live.
Here we find roots, spread wings.

WINONA
(Indian maiden on a cliff, forbidden to marry the man she loves)

Here, where Mother Valley spreads herself wide
For the Father of Waters to find his seamless way,
The sunset colors are so beautiful
They send shivers through bluffside trees.

Here in this high lovely calm
All customs and tribes have rainbow hues,
And four winds assign no blame
For the conspiracies of prejudice and pain
Woven into the frames of village life.

Here the heart's high priestess, serenity,
Gives sky permission
To marry water and earth.

So here, where property is a momentary rite
Practiced equally by those who fly,
I make my last stand,
My last will and testament,
My final step a leap, not a fall.

WINDUP

Another summer gone
Without one baseball thrown.
What do we know better
Than that wheel of memory,
The slow rocking to start us off,
Sinews gathering, arms pausing high
To praise the round windup of spring
Before the rearing back begins, then
The unfurling of boy sprung
From flesh curling in on itself?

PASTIME

A girl, nine years of wonder
Still on her face,
Stands directly on the bag at third
Running amazed fingers along the wrinkles
Of my old leather mitt.
It is the bottom of the ninth,
And everywhere in the world
The bases are loaded.

Beds of Leaves on Forest Floor

SEPTEMBER SONG

Now we are living in the last days.
The Book of Revelation commands
The Four Horsemen, manes moiling
In the curls of mushroom clouds,
To head our way. And space seers
Sense the light-year attraction
Galaxies have for yawning black holes.
And God knows how long
Before we will wilt
In our greenhouse beds.

    So now

We wave farewell to Mom and Dad
In a doorway alone,
And a neighbor walks by, and now
A daughter turns a corner toward school.
And one thing is certain now:
October light is almost here
And gone. Certainly
In the last days we are living now.

BLIND DATE

A sandstorm tears through downtown streets.
Widows walk backward to church.
Gargoyles spit on passing crowds.

On highway shoulders roadkill raccoons
Are deaf and dumb, ear to the ground.
Why are they cluttering our roads, listening?

Filthy water sits in the sink.
Can you shoot it up a tower of some sort?
I want you to clean up your mess.
You want me to clean up your mess.

I turned the TV off, I swear,
But it turned itself on.
Leave me alone, please,
But love me, or else.

The geese, ahead of the snow,
Suddenly fly north.
Let's not talk. Let's make a date.
9-11. I'll be there.

DECLARATION OF WAR

We'd better just do it because
The bottom is falling out
Of our shopping bags
And cows everywhere give too much milk
And our rockets alone
Drone on with our prayers
And the rains keep falling on Iowa fields
So we have too much corn to burn
And we need to be more certain
All the time to be afraid
Before it's too late because
Because the freeways are bloody full
Of cars obedient to One Way signs
And there's no going back
And no exit in sight.

THE FALLEN IN BATTLE

If we begin to see over time
Only those spoils strewn in the fields
Stretching from Marathon to Stalingrad,
We begin to lose sight
Of all but one:
Leg thrown carelessly aside,
Arm twisted behind his back,
Face up, his mouth not opened or closed,
As if caught in the act of speech.

All there, he has nothing now—
Not mother, lover or wife
Rank or name, no
Not one saleable souvenir
And no views
About death
As conservative
Or too liberal.

RECREATIONS
(For Tom Dukich, Mentor)

In the beginning, the second creation
Of the infinities still to come,
The one that burst into being
When the earth was without form
And darkness was on the face of the deep
And all was void save the ether of hydrogen:

Then the new old multiverse was delivered
Of its heavy elements—carbon, oxygen, iron, *et cetera*—
And there was light
On the firmament aswirl with iron-cored galaxies
Of stars, moons, a planet
And a kitchen sizzling with the fragrance
Of garlic in olive oil
Where Nona seasoned her cast iron skillet
With a rainbow sheen of bacon grease
And declared, "Let there be Italian meatloaf!"

Because no one is permitted
To eat any god raw in dining halls
Presided over by clocks conspiring
To arrest the moment that eats me.

There we recited the catechism
While Nona waved her wooden spoon like a wand:
Who made you? God made me.
Why did God make you? To show forth
Goodness and mercy in an iron skillet, crucible
Cast from the hot cores of stars
For the purpose of cooking up a third creation scene
Featuring Nona's witchery,

Her skillet the womb where the matters of life—
Milk-soaked ciabati, wafer-thin,
And parmigiano of young cow

Heal the broken body of the lamb
Perfumed by garlic in hot olive oil
In the shade of rosemary and oregano leaf—
These conspire to commit hot-fire alchemy
So that we, savoring the heavenly, may be reborn.

RECIPE

When my lover says I'm never glad,
Never cry, what's eating me,
I explain it's a matter of taste,
Bitterness gorging root, stem and leaf.
I tell her Events is a bully
Dumping all over us,
And I take it personally.
Outrageous, since even I know
What's eating stupid Events.
I tell her I've learned to love
Mustard greens fried in garlic and olive oil,
The heap spiked by wine vinegar.
They really make me go.

GREAT BATTLES OF THE CENTURY

The mothers are sweeping the fields,
Their eyes down looking for holes
Deep enough to bury the waste
Bequeathed by obedient sons.

Everywhere diapers are strewn, and muddy shoes,
And sweat-stained collars and shirts,
And beliefs abandoned like toys on the floor
After fathers got lost in strange streets.

The arms are there too, and wide-open mouths
With nothing to say about honor and truth,
Mothers alone now with love too drained
To plant any field with new grain.

SO GARDENS DIE

So gardens die, October battlefields
Carnage-strewn, all lines
In disarray after the plundering,
Wreckage of husks and seeds skull-dry
Under thread-bare weeds.

Only sky moans here
For muted skeletons,
Their bones bared to winds
Ghost-dancing hymns
Over tattered bodies still
Unburied and unharvested.

AN ESCHATOLOGY

"Will you die soon?" my son
Asked, wondering
How really really old sixty is
If he is too too already five
And therefore almost fifty too.

Not in a day, I say,
Or a year, this year
Or next or ever really
In the grave sinking fear
Mind knows
But heart never fully feels.

We there will live forever, we two,
You in me and I in you.

PERFUMES

Near her chamber,
Her door wholly ajar,
The fragrance of fall hay
Dizzied my brain.

As she came near
I felt my breath taken away
By a windrush that stirred
The wildflower of her form.

Her air primes the lowdown pulse.
Everyone lives inside everyone else.

JANE FONDA WORKED OUT

When our troubling Jane, working things out,
Recanted her romantic flight to Hanoi,
Her partying to unnatural political acts,
What kind of red did old veterans still see
In this unforgivable new Helen of Troy?

Did they image a plain Jane humped down:
Dowdy, doggy and fifty-one,
From some Toledo, Salinas or Keokuk,
Commonest daughter of working man
Suffered by veterans of all the wars
To bitch in the kitchen her bit about peace
When far out of sight and out of mind?

Or was she still Barbarella bombshell made
In the Hollywood factory of dreams, commodity
Drawn to the cover of *Self*, actress used
To be taken again, and born to model her lines?

When the bombers doubted over Hanoi
Above the mad elegy of siren screams,
Was she one face of an enemy dreamed,
The one not under but *in* the bed?

STRIP-SEARCH

As I stand undone in a window watch
Gazing at leaves falling to their doom
From limbs shadowed in light
While blame-tongued talk
Turns toward the nature of evil again,
The rule of nakedness requires me to strip
All uniforms from arms
And neighbors' smiles to white bone.

Where in the world is God
That this miracle should happen again
So quietly and as out of sight
As stolen love behind prison walls
Invisible from the county road
Where trucks gorged with rivets and milk
Speed past the cries
Of loons, mothers, and lost sons?

OCTOBER DAY

And there are moments, nameless,
Of clarity all sky, uncrossed
By bird or cloud, so still
We review that which was
Yet to be, as if all is here,
Now, a singular blues,
Longed for like a future
Abandoned
To mindlessness and chill winds.

FOUR FREEDOMS

1.
In a cathedral he saw his place of work:
At the end of a long well-polished corridor
Belief narrowed to a point.
As he shrank
He came to a door.

2.
From out of his chest
Creeping things came forth—
Toads, lizards, snakes, scorpions.
What damned fullness, he said,
What grays and browns,
What sun-shined skins.

3.
Night swallow,
Tilt-winged indeterminacy
Of all but flight,
Confident, playful, she streaks.

4.
Against the surfaces of flesh
Holding him in,
He pressed, balancing.

IF THINE EYE OFFEND THEE

Then the beauty in the beholder's eye
May be blurry, cruel, or astigmatized,
And crafts no line between what is liked
And worth our love.

These—
The sway of autumnal woods
Dancing in a deep blue sky,
Or jar poised on a hill,
Round, empty and complete,
Its weight a silent tone distilled
By the swift salutation
Of a tilting swallow's wing—

Differ in kind from dollar signs
Drawn from megawatts that cross the sky
With a cacophony of lines,
Or from the lyrics of a girl's fuck you shrilled
Across a deep blue summer pond.

When beauty is uncozzened by relativity
It charms the mind's concentric powers
To deepen into forms
The contours of radiance.
Never for sale are those rare eyes
With hands in them
That caress a wrinkled face
As they hold and turn the earth,
Afraid to let it drop.

STILL LIVES

The
word
still
haunts,
enduring
yet
motionless

The
motionless
still
haunts,
enduring
yet
word

Enduring
yet
motionless
still
haunts
the
word

Enduring
yet
haunts
the
motionless
still
word

Word
yet
motionless,
the
enduring
still
haunts

Enduring
yet
haunts
the
motionless
word
still

Motionless
yet
word,
enduring
haunts
the
still.

NUNS' CEMETERY

Your headstones turn their backs
To the tourists who can't hear
The silence you've achieved.

Here bees are dizzied by the blooms
That once were the faces of young girls.
Here spirits hide absence in dead air.

God gains weight in this green space.
Here the longed-for Son goes to seed
With wild grass, wayward flowers, and weeds.

WEEDS
(Grazie to Gerard Manley Hopkins)

The thistle and thorn, the ragweed dress
Shredded by hail and ratted by rain
Beworms the mud moiled in the plain
In loam cropped bare to the bone
While tongue, skull-numbed, is dumb
To Adam, red clay and words—

So let them be left,
Oh let them be left, the weeds
And the words,

The thistles and thorns, and Eve
On the leaf bristling with verse—
Oh let them be left, all wild and wet!
Long live the earth in her ragweed dress!

LATE AUTUMN REPAIRS

Cold rains repair worst and best,
Slicking down beds of leaves on forest floor
Before winds give a few leftover colors
Their final turn in the sun.

The shack, made of old boards
(Fir beams hauled out of some old man's dump,
And windows glazed from so much looking out),
Sags in such rain; abandoned
Old lumber rough as bark
Is slippery with cold mildew and mold.
Surely the joists will bend
Under the weight of so much sky,
And the door will become unhinged,
And the footings, losing their hold,
Will slide into the tarn of compost
The forest silently secrets deep down.

In the city we doubt
The shack will survive.
Composed, we conclude there comes a time
Not to repair there, a time to let things go,
Let the roof leak, the paint chip away
For the winds to get through.
Let the whole bottom inexorably fall out.

Something there is that does not love old shacks,
That sends cold rain before the frost
To soften bones and harden
Reluctance to repair
Loose shutters clapping wildly in wind.

The bottom of the ninth

THE DAY THE ROLLERCOASTER STOPPED

In Disney World,
At the peak of Thunder Mountain,
With thousands in line waiting their turns.

We all know how it's supposed to go:
The engine's mad right turn at the start,
Just before the slow dull climb
Just before the sudden fall.

But right at the top it stopped
Short of the lookout to the other side.
Three days before Christmas,
With the barometer steady
And skies fair as swans in flight.

No one in line knew right then
The lights in Tampa's airport also failed,
The doors of its monorail jammed, and
Inexplicably, TVs went on the blink
In St. Petersburg, while Michigan-made cars
Refused to run in the cold,
And a radar screen on the Arctic Circle
Showed rhythmical flutterings.

A boyish voice explained it all:
A computer had miscalculated.
The little engine couldn't for now.
It was necessary for everything to suspend.

A few lifted their voices to complain,
But the majority waited for another train.
Those who had never seen a swan
Could not imagine grounded flights
Or crossed computers eagle-eyed
For enemies invading through frozen skies
As down-like dots on a screen.

EMPTY COUNTRY CHURCH

From the blacktop road, or from the tombstones
Huddled half-buried in snow beneath a dogwood choir
Whistling wind's weird hymns,
No strangers track to your doors.

Only God sneaks in during work day hours,
A homeless gent hunched in a wool overcoat,
Face hidden from view as if afraid of being named,
Wondering how in the world things went so wrong

While you stand your ground, your red brick walls
A mind made up of hard-core belief
Proclaimed every Sunday on the hour
By a bell now mum with untold tales.

Your Sunday citizens—their weddings and funerals—
Are absentees in this house of representatives, gone
To cast to the winds their life and death votes.

Absence is here, and noiseless vacancy.
This space where the world is not at war
The solitary self fills with its serene insignificance.

And here, where the arguments souls have with minds
Are given the benefit of all doubts,
Leftover prayers that ascend like fog
Still circulate in search of a ceiling crack.

"I LAY MY CASE BEFORE HIM"
(John Berryman and Job 23:4)

J.B., drunk poet,
Tried his patience
A final time,
Waved to a puzzled old man,
And flew from the Washington Street Bridge.

He drifted on
No visions of Huck Finn:
No floating down the River
Dizzied by the Milky Way.

For in the land where he fell
No devils bet with gods.
The sky is frozen here,
The River like a stream of steel.

They say blood froze
In the silence of his fall,
And the laughter of lovers
Turned cold.

They say there was more to him
Than bones,
But in his case I divined
No longer dream, nor songs.

WAGNER'S VALKYRIE OVER STALINGRAD

When the Stuka music failed
The German boys at Stalingrad,
Leaving nothing behind
But the shrill white silence
Of frozen Russian skies,

Impossible then any return
To sporting on schoolyard grass
Where evil and good breezed right
Beyond spring's green songs.

From there they marched in anthem beat
To the steppes of no return,
Those feet suddenly by choice
Numbed against their wills.

Still undreamed the leveled waste
Of flesh freezing alone,
Or wind whistling its tunes
Through horrified bones.

AFTER THE LOGGING

The carnage is bloodless and cold,
The winter work of some sharp blade,
Entitled, for the sake of new ties,
To lop off limbs, slice trunks,
Leave everything strewn in the snow.

The logs lie still on bare hillside,
Rough full bodies, like strong women
Sleeping in the sun, beneath their skin
Clean flesh still fragrant in frozen air.
After the land lord has exercised his right, his
jus primae noctis, in full daylight,
No one dares ask
If trees have standing now.

Their dead-weight girth answers for them:
Once these matrons swayed in wind,
Did daily rounds in sun and rain,
And whispered aeolian evening songs.
Once their arms prevented storms,
Gave weight to roots
Unable to release their grip on earth,
Made crosses lighter to bear
And held up the sky.

OF MAPS

It is said he was given to sighs:
The philosopher Descartes transfixed
By any woman in a crowd
With crossed eyes.

He scoped, surveyed her place,
Charted the longings of her gaze
Past the walls of China and Berlin
Back to her face

Invisible behind black veils
In the marketplace of Kashmir
Where body and mind meet
To whisper their tales

About snakes sidling with doves
In the parallax of earth and stars,
Because flesh knows in its mind
That lust owns love.

We therefore draw our lines
Straight as the earth is round.
We think, therefore we are confused,
Moving on yes, groping
Wide-eyed for signs.

THE RIDDLE OF THE SPHINX

Why is it he learned too late
The earth's an alien chunk
Whose straightest lines never meet
In bottomless tangles of nerves,

Or therefore why

He's expected to walk tall
Wobbling on stilted premises
Over all the holes in arguments,
Knowing he is doomed to slip and fall
On probability curves?

CIRCULATIONS

In the beginning, until 1834,
Geologer Symmes swore the seas
Flowed into and out at the poles,
So balance was sustained at the core
Of an earth wobbling in place
While performing small wheelies in space.

The moon was wholly in tune with this scheme
Before books elbowed each other off racks
And squatters weighed down with gravity lines
Inspired fences to leap over migrant backs.

So now the slime afloat in seaside soup
Has nowhere to go but up,
With its blue cheeses and fat beefs
Gifted to bowels fogged with taste
In the absence of drains.

We wait for old rains.

JESUS AT HOME

When he returned to his door
From nights in a random street,
He had the irrepressible habit
Of crying himself to sleep.

Mary was too young to maintain control,
And the father, in his confusion,
Was generally dead to the world.

As new days dawned, he especially cared
For his eye-shadows, hair, and teeth,
And the fingernails he tore on wood, slivers
So hard on his hands, though
He loved nothing more than the way
Olive, once-shaved clean, was girl-smooth.

Everyone accused him of mixing
Water and wine, spilling
From the jar weighing him down.
He ate his share of bread,
But believed it was wrong
For saffron to take the edge
From lamb. Word traveled
About his unusual tastes,
Women were carried away,
Men taken by the beauty of his words
And face.

But who did he think he was?
There were holes in his arguments,
And somebody had to put a stop
To the bloody way he played
The wife, mind unmoved
As she stands by the unwashed bowls
After a feast, cheeky as hell,
Saying hit me again, you beast.

THE THIRD GIFT

John Rutter (composer) to Louis DeGrazia (theologian),
following the performance of Rutter's *Requiem* at the First
Plymouth Congregational Church in Lincoln, Nebraska:

> *"I'm afraid I have not been given the gift of faith.
> Nor have I been given the gift of happiness."*

As we stare at walls
And the one unopened door
With our instruments still untuned,
It is too soon to know
That gifts are the givers given to us.

The people enter the Cathedral
From the other side of that door,
Certain only of their uncertainty
As they file in to find their place
In this shrine given to making old music
New, heard again for the first time.

A choir of housewives, lovers and petty thieves
Also parades in from that door—
All robed in the uniform of absurd need
To make good music of tough times.

So John, what's lost if two birthday gifts
Unravelled as you composed your life?
When mad violence falls on children's heads
With noise orchestrated by the silence of God,
What presence were you given to create
Into a requiem for the death of belief
A wonderful new argument from design?

When your raven music airs death, it sings—
And when it ends even death has wings.

CHRISTMAS CAROL 1999

Following "There Is No Rose,"
Medieval carol anonymously composed,
The Blue Heron Consort
In the Chapel of the Angels
Sings Pierre Sandrin's "Doulce Memoire"
As evening shadows fall outside.

"Doulce memory in pleasure consumed,
O century which causes such knowledge,
Good and evil. Virtue will break its fame.
My honest hope of duty is to be
An example of doulce pleasure consumed."

The lyrics rise into a dome
Gilded by Byzantine mosaics
Gleaming over a lithe crucifix
Standing on air above white altar stones.

Gray-haired thoughts,
Good and evil too heavy for words,
Rise into the dome, circling there like birds
Looking for a way out.
O century, its infamy,
Which causes such memory.

Virtue will break
As blank-faced Mary ignores my prayer,
Gazing beyond the Jesus child in her lap.
My honest hope of duty is to be doulce.

Such sadness in the gathered beauty of this place,
The golden confusion aswirl in this shrine
To God's mind, incandescent dome,
Light lyrics brushing its hard tiles
Like airs off wings,
The last red petal of the last red rose
Not falling but rising into it,
Double pleasure consumed.

DAY AFTER CHRISTMAS

It's quiet where I sit staring out.
Trucks turn the corner and are gone,
Carting axels, rivets and oil
To the cities of carelessness.

Here, in this solitude, renewal ages
Comfortably within sight of the tree
Cut from another winter of our discontent
Now frozen into another new year of war.

Peace on earth roosts and broods here.
The few of us permitted this quiet
Are the overwhelming majority self-consoled,
Hands useless in our laps, hearts voting yes.

MOVING WITHOUT THE BALL
(The basketball addict speaks)

Ponderous,
These 64 year-old legs:
Still dreaming before they think
They leap, too late
To see who scored on him
Again.

There is only one way to play:
Give it up—
Keep the ball moving, buoyant
As the balloon-dreams of boys
Still dribbling between their legs.
Think it through.

The grave thing
Always in your face
Is hardest to chart:
The numbness
Defying gravity,
Working its way up
While the heart
Still skies.

RAINBOW MAN

When you nestled yourself, blue-blanketed,
Next to me that frozen day
And lifted your eyes to speak,
Your words descended like down on my bones:
    "Dad, tonight I saw you in my dream
      Standing on the rainbow in the sky."
I covered you then with my wing
To keep the vision safely in,
And when you closed your eyes again
The window frost turned crystalline.
Inside the dollhouse of your dream,
The other side of a looking glass,
You, still blue-blanketed,
Feared no frozen silent sky.

You see your five winters still that way:
Your blanket's blue, brilliant as clean August sky,
Wind's rhythms easy as the flight of white birds,
The snow warm, sweet, edible,
And therefore, plausibly, ordinarily,
I as mere blue man
Alone in a magic sky.

So I let you sleep, let the dull morning freeze,
Allow you to conjure me more remarkably: see me,
The prince wafted by translucent horse
Toward castle made of glass,
Or sky-giant, hoarder of sunset gold,
Or genius circling with Saturn's rings,
Or swan-god in love with girl's blond hair.
All these, greater I therefore am,
Than man in blue, mere rainbow lord.

For now your view will have to do—
Like this mere cold,
This gray sleep where stories take effect,

This shrinking and ungodly man.
It too will have to do—your soon forgetting
Once you said, "Dad, tonight I saw you
In my dream standing
On the rainbow in the sky."
And it will have to do—
This bare arm still covering you.

HOME ALONE

Where in the world am I better off
Than here, in this body tired of rectitude
As it shrinks toward the quietude
That makes breathing a privilege

Dully felt when the heart wearies
Of its mindless routine and warns the lungs
To keep pace with only slow songs—
Because the lease is up, though I own the house

That will outlive me, my children too,
This table and chair, this small space
Where I alone do a no-dance in place,
Thankful for now, still able to feel

Affection for words I offer late
To approve of this scarecrow still here.

RETIREMENT HOW-TO

Start empty: Look forward to nothing now,
Seeing there nothing but now.

Mark your age not from your date of birth,
But from the presumed end of the line
That leaves you endless moments to conceive
The life you dream.

Abandon all work ye who enter here.
Win by playing your way.

And be certain to leave the door open when you take off
So the young MBA's can wade in
To the full depth of their shallowness.

As you steal away turn a blind eye at bores
Churning in the bigwheel ruts of progress they make.

Then get out of town on the very first train,
The slow one with seats facing the caboose
And a widening expanse of receding fields
Green as the future you once looked forward to
When food was fragrant because it knew slow growth.

The sunset view will owl-eye you,
Your pupils dizzied as they fall in love
With ponds, trees, hills and the illegible sky
Where again, amazed, you misread the meaning of life.

In window reflections look for your father's face,
The black and white photo as blue as the gray
Lake Michigan waters you swam as a boy
Those sun days when time was not
Crawling inside classrooms and clocks.

Be sure to see that you will always forget

How empires and hemlines fall
Because of a flaw in the fabric of things
So wonderfully complex and intricately webbed
Your life comes to a single inarticulate point.

When food is served mull it slowly,
Savoring the fact that all tastes
For music, politics, women and art
Have their uses and may be enjoyed.

This requires you to pity and pardon all sinners equally,
For you know not what you do.

And because you will be toothless soon
Don't bare your fangs
When you turn the other cheek.

PALIMPSEST

Against the hieroglyphs drawn
By the black branches of plum
And its snow-whitened limbs
On my window at dawn,

A cardinal alights, red as sin,
And stands for song.

Mute as thoughts that fail to sound
The bird's serenade circulates in my mind
The histories of hope and despair
Untouched by words forced from my pen.

Song's traces are invisibly inscribed
Onto the blank spaces of the page,
The unspoken there eloquent white noise
Composed to silence the silences of God.

SNOW DAY

Here holy days descend from the north,
Blizzards delivered by white winds,
The special blessings of polar gods.
Everything is purified by such winds,
Roofs, highways, prairie fields swept,
Windows that have seen too much.
Through them the face of earth
Goes blank, a sheet pulled over its brow.

Then we turn in to white nights.
There, a low steady glow endures,
Too small to give great worry or pain.
And a pulse goes bump in the night,
Proof that one friendly fool
Lives still in the house—ghost
Indifferent to work piling up,
Requiring no more than hot soup,
A piece of bread, a taste of wine.
Then we call time out and in
And resign our hands to helplessness,
Suddenly grateful again.

THE THIRTEENTH MONTH
(A sonnet triptych)

I.
Weeds, groping for cracks in concrete,
One by one go deaf, dumb and blind.
Birds swallow refrains they can't repeat,
And in city air dawn loses her mind.
Baseball calls itself out this year,
Wars don't thaw on frozen fields of dreams,
And kids, unsafe at school, live at home in fear.
Earth's curveball spin, wound up by storms, seems
Undone, a knuckleball, berserk and blank.
And in these bankrupt times when bottom lines
Can't be rounded off, and when no bloated bank
Can calculate returns for wholesale crimes,
We doubt spring will come round again.
For the thirteenth month we have no name.

II.
For minds longing to believe what they know
And for eyes full of feelers for the unseen,
The earth performs its small routines offscreeen
Without betraying the secrets of her show.
How does the moon know when the time is right
To sway the tides closer to the sun
So waters can warm soil in silent night
And tendrils can begin their quiet run
Toward the dandelion, the old sun's rune
Rewritten on the schoolgirl's open face
Amazed at blossoms offering their white grace
To the lunatic leer of the naked moon.
For what spring brings round there is no name
When the thirteen month returns again.

III.
There is no respinning this old news.
Nature's gospel peters out, unleaving
The Book of Revelation to what we choose
By cheering on its chariot Lord, wheeling
His high-horsed revenge from sky on mad steeds
That obey the commands of a trumpet blast
Tuned to scorch the earth of all misdeeds,
Once and for all, present, future, and past.
It spawns a wide-screened movie in a small mind,
This cold-hate rescue full of fiery sounds,
This promise—that damns good folk left behind—
Redundant as sun making its rounds,
And current as thirteenth month without a name,
Rite of spring that will come round again.

THE MEANING OF LIFE

A blank page unriddles the certain
Annihilation of my scrawl, I, me,
Four-footed once, soon three,
And once upon a time two,

Pulsar whose velocity of nouns
And direction of verbs
Amount in all probable uncertainty
To nothing more lovely

Than passage past azaleas
Into the Ireland of your eyes
That have one significant thing to do
With a mother walking with her child
On a safe, familiar street.